Nottingham Railway Sta

C000229374

on old picture postcards

Brian Lund

1. Nottingham Midland station interior on a postcard published by Albert Hindley in 'Clumber' series no. 268, about 1905. The bridge carrying the Great Central line from Victoria to Arkwright Street is prominent in the picture.

Designed and Published by
Reflections of a Bygone Age,
Keyworth, Nottingham
1991

Printed by
Adlard Print and Typesetting Services,
Ruddington, Notts.

ISBN 0 946245 36 3

Acknowledgements: Illustrations 6, 13, 20, 31-33, 40, 45-49, 51-53 reproduced courtesy of Lens of Sutton; nos. 8-9, 43-44 courtesy of H.B. Priestley.

2. W.H. Smith's bookstall at **Nottingham Victoria** on a c.1906 card. Note the postcard rack in the left foreground. WHS published their own cards of railway stations though this one is by an unidentified photographer.

INTRODUCTION

The coming of the railways in the nineteenth century revolutionised social life, bringing speed and efficiency to the delivery and transport of all kinds of goods, milk and dairy produce, mail and newspapers. Opportunities for personal travel were immediately widened, though this benefit only filtered through gradually to all sections of society. Railway-building brought out a whole range of differing reactions, from outright opposition from many landowners who didn't want the new invention riding across their estates, to delirious enthusiasm from businessmen and municipal officials who could see the benefits that railways might bring. In fact, for a town or village to be on the railway network became a status symbol. To be missed out was to risk being left behind in the Middle Ages.

If the railway system of Britain had been centrally planned and better organised, it might have become more prosperous and lasted longer. But different lines were built by competing individual companies and privately funded, and rivalry often meant duplication of routes. Stations, especially village ones, were often inconveniently situated because of problems of geography, cost, or local landowner opposition. Sometimes stations were built to serve two communities and sited in between, with difficult access for both.

Nottingham got on the network early, courtesy of the Midland Railway Company, but managed to miss out on a direct main line route to London, taking second place to Derby (Midland) and Newark/Grantham (Great Northern).

Eventually, the Midland built its own direct route via Melton in 1882, and then the Great Central opened up the heart of the city to provide what was intended to be the new super-line to the capital. It was too late, though: there were now four lines to London from the East Midlands, and the age of road transport was beckoning. Competition from rival lines, and from buses and motor cars, caused headaches for all the main companies. The heyday of rail travel and company profitability, 1880-1910, evaporated with two world wars and Austin-Morris.

The host of large and small companies that had built the railway network were merged into four in 1923, and nationalised as British Railways in 1947. The following twenty years saw wholesale closure of lines and stations as government sought frantically to make the system less of a public burden.

Nottinghamshire was extremely well-served by rail (or hopelessly over-networked, depending on your point of view), though much of this was designed for goods traffic rather than a desire to provide a passenger transport system. Bulwell residents, for instance, could choose from five stations! In 1910, three lines ran north in parallel from Nottingham to Sutton-in-Ashfield, and three different companies met at the remote Langwith Junction.

This book is not a detailed resumé of the history of each station in the county, but rather snippets of pictorial nostalgia. The choice of illustrations has been governed solely by what postcards were available. The boom years for picture postcards were 1902-14, and, like the railways, were produced by private individuals and firms. Thus, coverage of local landmarks like stations was haphazard, and the only three publishers whose work appears in any quantity here are W.H. Smith, Albert Hindley ('Clumber' series) and J.H. Scott. Several later photographs with postcard backs are included, too. Publishers are acknowledged where known, but often remained anonymous. Date of postal usage of the postcards is also given where relevant.

Curiously, it is not the biggest stations which are easiest to find on postcards: Nottingham's Victoria and Midland interiors, and the Mansfield duo are rare on cards, while Netherfield, Gedling, and Bingham appear relatively frequently. I hope this selection will prove an enjoyable one for railway fans and Nottinghamshire residents.

Brian Lund, February 1991

> 490

3. Beeston station, an important first step on the Midland main line, nine minutes from Nottingham by the inaugural train on this line in 1839. Card published by W.H. Smith (their bookstall is on the right) about 1910. Beeston is featured on many postcards – far more, in fact, than Nottingham Midland or Victoria.

4. Stapleford and Sandiacre station, between Long Eaton and Ilkeston on the Midland line. This card by local photographer Marrin shows the sloping exit tunnel to reach the road and station buildings. It was posted from Stapleford in October 1906. Stapleford station closed to passengers in January 1967.

5. An unusual view of **Ruddington** on the Great Central, showing the typical G.C. pattern of lines at either side of the main platform. In Edwardian days the station served a village with a population of about 2,500 and seventeen trains in each direction stopped on weekdays. Ruddington lost its passenger service on 4th March 1963, some six years before the entire line closed. No indication of the publisher of this 1920s postcard.

Rushcliffe Halt Station & Marblite Works, East Leake.

6. Rushcliffe Halt, the next station southbound down the line, closed on the same day. It had been put up to serve the marblite (now British Gypsum) works at East Leake. Moves are afoot to link up the old G.C. line from Ruddington to the preserved section run by the Main Line Steam Trust at Loughborough.

7. A Midland compound steams into **Plumtree** with a Nottingham-bound train in the late 1920s. Milk churns on the platform are ready to be loaded onto the train, and there is a useful number of passengers. But the station, which served both Plumtree and Keyworth, hardly survived the second world war: it closed to passengers in February 1949; goods traffic was maintained until 1965.

8. **Plumtree** was one of the stations on the Midland Railway's direct line to London via Melton Mowbray, opened in 1880. By the time this photo was taken of 44817 on a London-bound express in the mid-fifties the station was long closed to passengers. The buildings now house a bistro, and the line is used as a British Rail test track.

9. Widmerpool, the next station up the line, had the same closure dates as Plumtree and has also been converted to a restaurant. It was always used primarily for goods traffic: the nearest village was a mile and a half away with a population of 158 at the turn of the century – hardly a promising basis for well-filled trains! Here 44186 is one half of a double-headed goods train around 1959.

10. Birds-eye photographic view of **Netherfield** station in 1913, a busy junction serving the main line to Grantham (opened in 1850) as well as local trains to Basford and Shirebrook.

COLWICK STATION. NOTTS

11. The same station on a 'Clumber' series card (no. 12) posted in February 1907. Bradshaw's railway guide referred to it as 'Netherfield' but the term **'Colwick and Netherfield'** was used to distinguish it from the Midland's Carlton and Netherfield.

RAILWAY STATION, RADCLIFFE-ON-TRENT

12. Radcliffe-on-Trent still serves passengers on the Nottingham-Grantham line as it did in 1913 on this 'Peveril Real Photo Series' card, no. 571. It's conveniently located near the village centre and has a current weekday service of 17 passenger trains each way; in 1910 it was only a few more, and that included services on the G.N./L.N.W. route to Melton.

THE G.N.R. STATION, BINGHAM.

13. The still-extant Great Northern station at **Bingham,** with plenty of activity on this c.1910 postcard, when the earliest weekday morning train into Nottingham was 7.30 a.m.

ASLOCKTON STATION.

14. Aslockton, next station on the same line, which also has an impressive service to-day. The ever-present milk churns on a c.1913 photographic card in the 'N.B.' series.

15. No trace remains of **Bingham Road** station on the Great Northern/London and North Western joint railway which meandered through the Vale of Belvoir to Melton Mowbray. A mile out of the village, it was the first station after the line branched off the Nottingham-Grantham track. Just five trains each weekday called here, and there was no Sunday service. Card published by E. Richardson, Market Place, Bingham, and posted from there in August 1917. *"I am going harvesting owing to the fact that men are awfully scarce"*, wrote Ted to his aunt in Paignton. Bingham Road closed in June 1951; it's now the start of a nature trail.

16. Barnstone station was next up the line from Bingham Road, serving the population of Langar-cum-Barnstone (485 in 1901). Its spacious buildings were very generous for such a rural station; it closed to passengers in 1953 and goods traffic in 1962. The card, written at Langar Hall, was posted in January 1912.

17. Burton Joyce on the Midland line from Nottingham to Lincoln, opened in August 1846. Like the other stations on this route, it is still open. 'Clumber' series card no. 174, posted at Manchester in November 1911.

18. Superb real photographic card of a train pulling into a crowded **Lowdham** station on a postcard by J.H. Scott of Bulcote, postally used in March 1908.

19. Another Scott of Bulcote card featuring **Thurgarton** station. In 1910 a dozen trains stopped most weekdays in each direction, with two on Sundays. The village still has twelve weekday trains, while the Sunday service shows five trains into Nottingham.

20. Rolleston was a junction station for Southwell and Mansfield until the Southwell branch closed in June 1959. This postcard by C. & A.G. Lewis of Nottingham dates from about 1923.

Bleasby

21. In 1901 **Bleasby's** population was 287, and they were well-served by the Midland railway. This card — again by Scott — was posted in June 1913, with the message *"This is our station, the 4.30 milk train just coming in. Everywhere is looking lovely. We went over the Trent on Sunday evening. Can get a glorious view for miles around."*

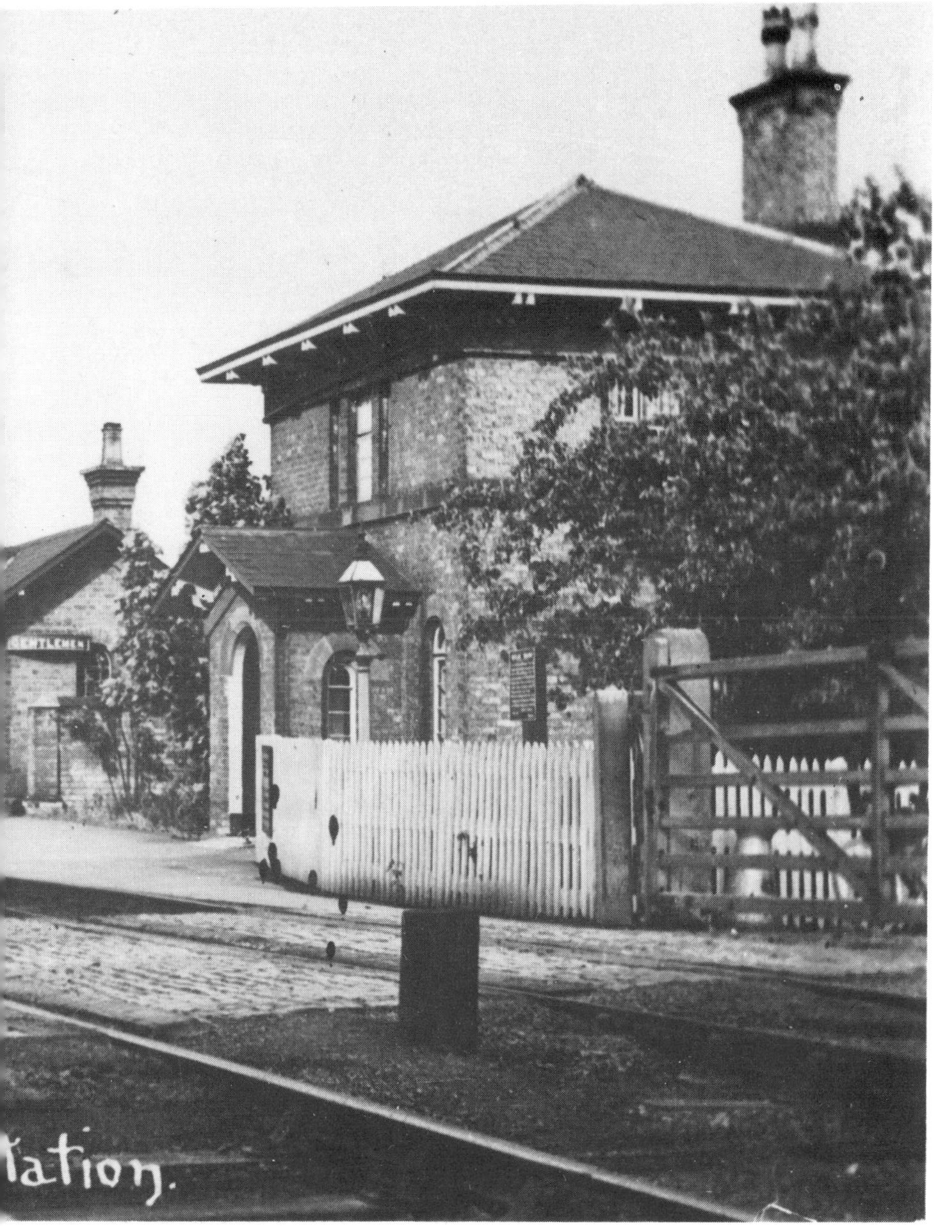
GENTLEMEN
tation.

22. Fiskerton station exterior. The village had a population of 369 in 1901.

23. Interior of **Fiskerton** with a train pulling away in the distance. Both this and the card above were by Scott of Bulcote. *"We are having a good time here"*, wrote Florrie, *"we went to Elston Church Sunday across the ferry."*

S 3042　　　　　　MIDLAND STATION. NEWARK

24. W.H. Smith postcard no. S 3042 of **Newark Midland** (now Newark Castle).

Great Northern Station, Newark

25. The more important **Newark** station was the Great Northern one on the main Kings Cross-Edinburgh line, seen here in 1908 on a postcard by Valentine of Dundee. It was posted in Newark to an address in Castle Gate in the town, with a note to say the writer would be *"down about 7 or 7.30 tomorrow."* – an indication of the way the postcard in Edwardian days was used in the same way the telephone is now.

26. Kirklington station was the first one out of Southw•
weekday (to Newark) and five (to Mansfield). The stati•
daughter Mary and posted at Blackpool in July 1911. Kir
trains in May 1964.

the Midland line to Mansfield and served by six trains each
ster and his family feature on this postcard, written by his
on closed to passengers on 12th August 1929 and to goods

27. One more stop along the line was **Farnsfield,** which also lost its passener service in 1929. Despite a population of over 900 at the turn of the century, it was unable to generate enough traffic to justify remaining into the thirties. Anonymously-published photographic card.

28. Mansfield's Midland station, a busy and thriving complex, providing services to Alfreton, Chesterfield, Newark, Nottingham, Worksop and Sutton-in-Ashfield. Despite this, services disappeared for good on 12th October 1964. Photographic postcard in the 'H H H' series.

29. Edwinstowe, on the Great Central's line to Lincoln through the Dukeries. Five staff are on hand in this 1916 postcard, used from the village in June that year. The station closed to passengers in January 1956.

30. Crow Park on the East Coast Great Northern main line lost its stopping passenger trains on 6th October 1958, and its goods services in 1964. This card, postally used from Sutton-on-Trent in 1920, was published by E.L. Scrivens of Doncaster.

31. The Great Northern station at **Tuxford**, 132 miles from Kings Cross on the main East Coast route, was closed to passengers in July 1955. Tuxford lost two railway stations within three months, as Tuxford Central closed in September. The level crossing immediately beyond the signal box carried the Tuxford-Lincoln road over the railway.

32. Dukeries Junction. The Great Northern station, threequarters of a mile south of Tuxford (G.N.) is most prominent, while above is the Great Central station of the same name, which served the Chesterfield-Lincoln line. Both these stations were closed completely in March 1950.

33. Whiteborough lay between Mansfield and Pye Bridge on the Midland Railway, and served the community of Hucknall-under-Huthwaite (population 4,076 in 1901). Referred to in Edwardian gazetteers and railway timetables as Whiteboro', it closed on 4th October 1926.

34. Ranskill on the Notts-Yorkshire border and the East Coast main line lay 5½ miles north of Retford, serving a 1901 population of 416. Passenger trains, mostly Retford-Doncaster locals, lasted until October 1958.

35. Nottingham Victoria's exterior rapidly became one of the city's landmarks, though opened only in May 1900. The closure of the station in 1967 after a relatively short life, and its conversion to a shopping centre, meant the destruction of all the frontage apart from the clock tower and the hotel. 'Clumber' series card no.351.

S 2540   INTERIOR VICTORIA STATION, NOTTINGHAM

36. Built by the Great Central, **Victoria** also accommodated Great Northern passenger trains which had previously used London Road station. This W.H. Smith postcard (no. S 2540) shows a view soon after the station's opening.

37. Thorneywood was one of three stations on the Nottingham suburban line, opened in 1886 to provide a commuter service into the city centre. Competition from trams meant it soon ceased to become viable, though, and its passenger service had only a thirty-year life, closing in 1916. Goods traffic on the line continued until 1951.

38. Sherwood station was the third on the suburban line (St. Anns Well was the second), and boasted substantial buildings, for the project to build the line – financed by Nottingham businessmen – was an ambitious one. 'Clumber' series card, unnumbered.

39. Another view of **Sherwood** station, taken at line level, on an anonymously-published photographic postcard, with Great Northern engine no. 241 approaching. The card was posted in the city in March 1910. Sherwood also closed in 1916.

40. Gedling and Carlton in 1912, with G.N. engine no. 66 on a Basford-bound train. Gedling was on a kind of 'outer ring' line, with the Basford-Daybrook-Gedling-Netherfield-London Rd. High Level-Victoria-Basford circular 10 miles long and taking about forty minutes.

41. Another view of **Gedling and Carlton** showing a clearer shot of the station buildings, looking towards Netherfield. The service lasted until 4th April 1960, when the station was completely closed.

MIDLAND STATION, BULWELL. NOTTINGHAM.

42. Bulwell could at one time boast four railway stations and a halt. This 'Peveril' series card (postally used at Barrow-on-Soar in August 1906) shows the Midland station, known as Bulwell Market and closed to passengers in October 1964. But there was also Basford & Bulwell (closed September 1964) and Bulwell Forest (September 1929) on the Great Northern, and Bulwell Hall Halt (May 1930) and Bulwell Common (March 1963) on the Great Central. All this may have been good for consumer choice, but it was typical of the expensive duplication of routes that helped bring all the passenger services down in the end.

43. Basford Vernon station on the Midland, closed in January 1960, and seen here the year prior with 48097 on a local goods.

44. Radford, on the Midland connecting line from Nottingham to Trowell, which closed in October 1964. This view is of mid-fifties vintage.

45. Annesley was on the Midland line from Nottingham to Mansfield via Hucknall, 11¼ miles out of the city. Serving a 1901 population of 1,271, it had eleven trains in each direction on weekdays (four more on Saturdays), and just a couple on Sundays. Passenger trains ceased in April 1953.

46. Sutton-in-Ashfield was also overburdened with railway stations, having four to its credit. This is the Midland's, which was a terminus in the town itself. Frequent services ran from here to Mansfield, with Sutton Junction, three-quarters of a mile up the line, providing a facility for changing to a train for Nottingham. Sutton Midland closed to passengers in September 1949.

47. The Great Northern station at **Sutton-in-Ashfield**, where passengers alighted for Huthwaite as well. Closure came here in September 1956, while this postcard dates from around 1912.

48. Sutton Junction on the Midland enjoyed a busy time in Edwardian days, with frequent services for passengers to Mansfield, Nottingham, and Pye Bridge. The station was closed in October 1964.

49. Langwith's population of 322 at the turn of the century had the facility of a railway station on the Mansfield-Worksop/Chesterfield Midland lines. Nine trains each weekday ran on the former route, five on the latter in each direction. Services were maintained until October 1964. This photographic card was posted at Mansfield in October 1905.

S 4884

RAILWAY STATION, WORKSOP.

50. Worksop station on W.H. Smith 'Kingsway Real Photo' series S 4884. Miraculously, it's still open, on the Sheffield-Lincoln former Great Central line. It served trains on this route and the Midland line to Mansfield until the latter was closed in 1964.

G.N. Station, Kimberley, Notts.

51. Kimberley's 5,000 plus population in 1901 *("a thriving place, carrying on coal mining, brewing and malting")* had railway stations on the Midland and Great Northern lines. The latter (Kimberley East) was on the Grantham-Stafford line, and also hosted a branch to Pinxton. Passenger services lasted until September 1964.

52. Kimberley West, the Midland's station, has an impressive array of six staff on this c.1905 postcard, when there were six weekday stopping trains in each direction (none on Sundays). Despite its impressive station sign (Kimberley for Watnall, Nuthall and Giltbrook: change for Pinxton), it was on a railway backwater, wandering into Nottingham Midland via Watnall, Basford, and Radford, and was never a viable route. The station was closed to passengers in January 1917, though goods traffic continued until 1951.

53. Kimberley Midland again, with crowds of schoolchildren on the platform and footbridge – school outing or royal visit? – about 1910.

54. Sturton station on the Retford-Gainsborough section of the Great Central, shown on a photographic card posted at Retford in June 1905. The station was built to serve the village of Sturton-le-Steeple (population 457 in 1901) and had seven stopping trains each way in 1910. Passenger closure came in February 1959, goods in April 1964.

The Village Railway Station

The railway network was a mass of contradictions and contrasts, with the atmosphere at Nottingham Victoria, for example, as far removed from Widmerpool or Edwinstowe as the M1 is from a country lane today. But all became part of the same interdependent network, and when branch lines were axed in the fifties and sixties, important feeder routes to the main system were lost. Nottinghamshire, like everywhere else, had its remote stations, but has been fortunate in retaining at least two cross-country lines — to Newark and Grantham — where village stations have remained open. Their character, however, has gone for ever: now they are staffless halts — at Bleasby and Elton, for example. Ninety years ago, though, when railways were the most frequently-used transport, the village station was often the life and soul — economic, social and political — of the community it served. It was *"part of the district it served, with its own natural history, its own legends and folk lore, a staff who were at the heart of village affairs, its stations and adjoining pubs, places for exchange of gossip, news and advice."**

The country stationmaster would be among the most respected of village citizens, if not the most popular. He and his staff (often half-a-dozen or more) took great pride in the appearance of their station and the efficiency of their service, which would include receipt of mail, newspapers and all kinds of goods, as well as the safe carriage of people. Many country stations had the telegraph installed as early as 1868. Rural stops handled milk, animals for market, farm produce, beer, grain and a host of other articles. With its own buildings, including waiting-rooms, booking hall, staff rooms, toilets, sometimes even a refreshment room, with a signalbox, possibly an engine-shed, with a yard for goods deliveries, a well-kept garden, and staff houses, country stations were often almost self-contained communities!

* *The Country Railway — David St. John Thomas*

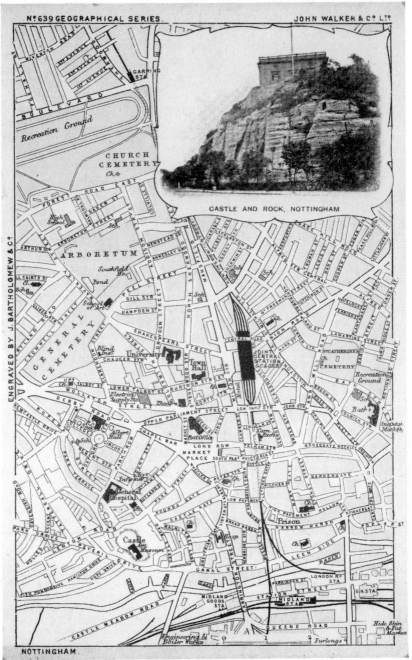

CASTLE AND ROCK, NOTTINGHAM

55. This map card published by John Walker of London shows Nottinghamshire's two main line stations, as well as London Road High Level, the old Great Northern station, the Midland goods station, and Carrington. It also demonstrates how the Great Central ploughed through the city centre, with tunnels under Huntingdon Street, Pelham Street and Victoria Street. Card published in 1904.